HOLSINGER'S CHARLOTTESVILLE

Rufus W. Holsinger
1866 – 1930

HOLSINGER'S CHARLOTTESVILLE

A Collection of Photographs by Rufus W. Holsinger

Cecile Wendover Clover *and* F. T. Heblich, Jr.
with an introduction by Bernard P. Chamberlain

All rights reserved, no part of this book may be reproduced in any form or by an electronic or mechanical means including information, storage and retrieval systems without permission in writing from the publisher, except by a reviewer who may quote brief passages in a review.

First Printing 1976
Second Printing 1978
Second Edition 1995

Library of Congress Catalog Card Number 76-46191
ISBN Number 0-9639374-5-6

Printed and Bound in Canada by D. W. Friesen & Sons Ltd.
Design by Diane Nelson

Art Restoration Services
P. O. Box 6701
Charlottesville, Virginia 22906
(804) 974-1726

Copyright 1976
Copyright 1978
Copyright 1995

*This book is dedicated
to the people of Charlottesville
for their appreciation of the past
and their faith in the future.*

❦ PREFACE ❦

THE READER SHOULD BE AWARE that this book is not a pictorial history in the sense that it does not follow chronologically, nor does it develop any themes. It is a book of pictures. The photographs contained herein were chosen at random, and the criteria used for selecting the photographs were simple. The authors of this book chose the photographs which they felt best illustrated what the city of Charlottesville and the people who lived in it were like some sixty years ago, and how different they are from today. In several cases, photographs were chosen to show how *similar* things are to our own times. Some pictures were selected because of their stunning beauty, and others were included for their amusement value. The authors had at their disposal some 9,000 photographs from which to choose, and less than 100 are reproduced between these covers. Some method of selection, how every arbitrary, was necessary and the authors offer no defense for any startling omissions which may have been made.

The organization of the book also presented several problems. It would have been possible to group the pictures according to theme: industry, commerce, entertainment, education, transportation, etc. However, many pictures would have been difficult to categorize under such a system, and several photographs would just as easily fall under any of two or more headings. Thus, a different approach was chosen. The photographs are presented in a geographical pattern, beginning with Michie Tavern and Monticello east of Charlottesville, traveling through the downtown business district, continuing down Main Street to the University, and ending in the western outskirts of the city. Consequently, the book, in this form, becomes something of a tour guide. The reader would do well to imagine himself as a visitor to Charlottesville in the early years of the twentieth century traveling this route, catching glimpses of the town and its residents.

The Holsinger Collection is unique in several respects. The fact that it survived for half a century virtually uncared for in the studio's basement is remarkable. Just how many of the glass negatives were broken or lost is unknown, and one can only speculate what images were lost with them. A portrait of Robert E. Lee is one certain casualty. Despite all this, though, the greater part of the Collection is intact and resides under the careful watch of the staff of the Manuscripts Division of the University of Virginia's Alderman Library where no bursting water pipe will ever foul its integrity.

The photographs in the collection are valuable not just because they are old, but because they are rare. Today nearly everyone has a camera of some sort, and if the Rotunda burst into flames again there would be thousands of photographs, not to mention movie film and videotape, recording the event. But in 1900 photography was the province of the professional and the serious amateur. Thus, the photographs that have been passed down to us are not only old and rare, but usually of remarkable high technical and artistic quality.

Charlottesville was extremely lucky to have a photographer like Rufus W. Holsinger. He mastered a difficult skill, and more importantly, he apparently had some concern for posterity. Many of the "historical" photographs were the product of routine business situations. As the leading photographer in town, naturally he was hired to photograph special events such as building dedications and statue unveilings. But even a brief perusal of the collection shows that some of the photographs were taken simply on whimsey.

Life was changing rapidly in America during this period, even in Charlottesville, and it is obvious that Holsinger sensed it. Things do not change overnight, and it was during this period that the old and the new co-existed; that the horse and buggy traveled side-by-side with the automobile and the trolley car. It is fortunate that Holsinger chose to record this period, the twentieth century in its infancy, for us.

Once the photographs were selected, it was decided that, when published, they should be accompanied by a narrative. It was further decided that the narratives should be limited to the specific photographs which they would accompany. Thus, nearly each page in this book stands on its own.

The authors soon discovered when they set off to research the photographs that very little in the way of a coherent history has been written about Charlottesville in the twentieth century. Consequently, much of the information in this book is "oral" history. Often this was the product of the authors, photograph in hand, shuffling through a neighborhood looking for the oldest person available. Though memories often fade, and imaginations replace them, it is believed that all of the information collected in this method is accurate. The other major source of information came from old newspapers which, though faded themselves, proved quite helpful. Where possible, the authors have reprinted verbatim accounts of special events in an attempt to add a bit of flavor to the narratives. If the reader gets the sense that some of the narratives are no more than bits and pieces of information loosely linked together, he is entirely correct. The narratives are intended to be informative and, occasionally, entertaining. There are, no doubt, inaccuracies in some of the text, but none deliberate. The authors apologize in advance for any errors and welcome any corrections or additions readers may offer.

Some people deserve special mention for the help they gave during the production of this book. Barbara Rushia, the manager of Holsinger Studios, and her assistant, Mary Kelergis diligently filled our requests for prints of the photographs, and helped in the selection process. Ralph Holsinger and Ethel Holsinger, the children of Rufus Holsinger, helped identify several of the photographs and offered useful information about others. Howard Newlon of the Virginia Highway Research Council provided much of the material about roads included in the narratives. Staff of the Reference Room of Alderman Library were most helpful in locating research sources for some of the more difficult and obscure subjects. And Bernard P. Chamberlain not only wrote the elegant introduction for the book, but saved the authors countless hours of legwork with his extensive knowledge of local history and remarkable memory.

Cecile Wendover Clover
F. T. Heblich, Jr.

❦ PREFACE TO THE SECOND PRINTING ❦

IT WOULD HAVE BEEN POSSIBLE for us to title this printing of *Holsinger's Charlottesville* "Second Edition" rather than "second printing" and keep clear consciences. Several changes have, indeed, been made in the book but not enough, we felt, to call the book a second edition or revised edition. To do so would have been to mislead those persons who purchased copies of the first printing into thinking they were missing something. They aren't, not much. We, the authors, were wrong about a few things, and we felt compelled to correct them when the book was reprinted.

The major change in this printing is the omission of the photograph identified in the first printing as the "Woolen Mills". While there is certainly a strong resemblance between the Woolen Mills building and the photograph, the photograph is not of the Woolen Mills. As best we know, it is of a power plant in Schuyler.

Also, we incorrectly identified the movie theatre (page 50) as the Jefferson Theatre. It is the Lafayette Theatre, owned by the company which owned the old Jefferson Theater. And, we have rewritten the caption for the Michie Tavern photograph to reflect historical accuracy.

Several minor changes, such as dates and spellings of names have been made in the introduction.

Many of these changes were brought to our attention by Velora Carver Thomson and we thank her for her concern for the town's history and her kindness in helping us record it accurately.

Holsinger's Charlottesville was first printed in 1976, the Bicentennial Year, and renewed interest in our nation's past seems to have renewed interest in the history of Charlottesville. In that same year John Hammond Moore's excellent volume, *Albemarle: Jefferson's Country, 1727–1976* was published by the Albemarle County Historical Society. A year later, long-time Charlottesville resident Joe Eddins published an entertaining booklet of sketches and reminisces called "Around The Corner, Just After World War I".

Also, since 1976 several places and people mentioned in the first printing of this book have become relegated to the realm of history. The most notable loss is that of Holsinger Studio itself. After several changes in management and ownership the photography studio, which chronicled the residents of Charlottesville and their town since the 1880s went out of business. We note the passing of the studio with great sadness, but the achievements of the studio and its two great photographers, Rufus Holsinger and his son, Ralph Holsinger, survive in the photographic images, captured for all time. Presently, the Holsinger Collection is being purchased by the Alderman Library of the University of Virginia. We are confident the new owners will endeavor to treat this great treasure with the affection it deserves and also act to make the collection more accessible to the public.

Cecile Wendover Clover
F. T. Heblich, Jr.
July 1978

❦ PREFACE TO THE THIRD PRINTING ❦

IT IS HARD TO BELIEVE that eighteen years have passed since the last printing of *Holsinger's Charlottesville*. Returning after all these years to the study of this book, the careful scrutiny of each photograph, has given me the same almost indescribable sense of romance that I felt when I found the collection over twenty years ago. I still feel the excitement like a mystery unfolding, as my elders guided me through a tour of their memories of our town. I have found that people empower the places they live by the way in which they live their lives. In days gone by I think they *knew* that—people *knew* who they were. Naturally we are affected by the energy of such intention in subtle, profound ways. This is a part of what makes this area so complex and interesting.

There is something about looking at these old photographs which conjures up heady feelings, transporting me to that other time when surely life went by at a slower pace, when surely people noticed one another and the events around them with a keener interest than today. I suppose the word is nostalgia. This desire to return to one's home, to earlier times, is thwarted for a number of longtime residents in that so much has physically changed for Charlottesville and Albemarle County. All there seems to be left for many of us are some wonderful photographs and our memories. Our memories are extremely important because they remind us of Who We Are, and where we came from, for better or for worse.

The process of creating the second edition of *Holsinger's Charlottesville*, (its third printing) turned into quite an undertaking, but one which offered the opportunity of considerably improving upon our first printing twenty years ago. Because of the time span between printings, I basically had to start from scratch as it were, and I want to thank the University of Virginia's Special Collections Department at Alderman Library as well as Pauline Page, of the University of Virginia's Printing Services at Alderman Library. The most important person to me in working with this project was my dear friend Diane Nelson, whose firm guidance gave me the confidence that it *could* be done gracefully, and who gave the book a "new and improved" look through her skill in layout and design. I want to thank Shanti Durkee and Susan Ida Smith for their help, as well as Lynwood Napier, who has always been supportive, savvy and helpful with so many of my endeavors. I also want to say how much I appreciate the kind help of Mr. Lionel Key, who went through *Holsinger's Charlottesville* with Mac and me just one more time, to check for any errors. Mac Woodward has been a pillar of enthusiasm for this project, enthusiasm which shall be counted on as we continue collecting the stories of Charlottesville and Albemarle County.

I think that the most wonderful difference in this edition is the fact that all of the photographs are improved in quality through printing them as duotones, which adds far greater visual detail. Also, you may notice the return of the page on The Charlottesville Woolen Mills, with its *correct* photograph. There have also been several minor changes made to update the book as well as additional photographs. If I have made an egregious mistake (or two, or more) I must ask you, dear fellow lovers of local history, to inform me. I hope that *Holsinger's Charlottesville* will continue to enrich the lives of our neighbors here in Charlottesville and Albemarle County by giving a glimpse into days gone by through the photographs of a remarkable gentleman, Rufus W. Holsinger.

Cecile Wendover Clover

❦ INTRODUCTION ❦

A FACE ONCE LAUNCHED a thousand ships. A picture speaks a thousand words. The communicating power of an image is inexhaustible. The best that words can do is to describe what is not visible in a picture or to relate the picture to an historical pattern or to some other interesting association.

This is a book of pictures and one can see in them what one wants to see. They were taken by Rufus W. Holsinger, the leading photographer of the Charlottesville area in the first quarter of the present century, and more especially in the five or ten years on either side of A. D. 1910.

The pictures appearing in this book were selected from the Holsinger collection to illustrate isolated instances in the life of the community in the foregoing period. The author of this introduction having lived in Albemarle County from 1896 to the present time will attempt to set forth a frame within which the various scenes may be visualized as representing bits in the history and development of Charlottesville.

Charlottesville—as nearly everyone knows—was arbitrarily laid out in a wilderness on either side of the Three Chopt Road in 1762, to be the second county seat of Albemarle County. When the county was reduced to approximately its present size in 1761 and the old county seat, Scott's Landing (Scottsville) was no longer near the center of the county, a new site had to be chosen for convenience, and a small hill lying between the Chestnut (Southwest) Mountains and the Blue Ridge was selected. A rectangle of 28 acres, four east-west streets, five north-south streets, 56 half acre lots, and a two acre public square for the Court House became the new county seat. It was named for the young wife of the Colony's reigning monarch, King George III. The fair Queen had been Princess Charlotte, of Mecklenberg-Strelitz, one of the Hanoverian principalities. The names of the east-west streets survive today—Jefferson, Market, Main (the Three-Chopt or Three Notched Road) and Water—but the expressive names of the six cross streets have yielded to "progress." Court is now East 5th, Union is East 4th, School is East 3rd, Church is East 2nd, Green is 1st, and Hill is West 2nd. And the first additional street, Maiden Lane, is now High Street. Again, with some degree of shame, Free Bridge Road is East High and Fry's Springs Road is Jefferson Park Avenue.

The growth of Charlottesville was slow, with most of the life centered around the Court House, north of Jefferson Street, where three presidents of the new nation, Jefferson, Madison and Monroe met and transacted business frequently. After Charlottesville was chartered in 1888 development was more rapid and the lovely residential streets, Park Street and Ridge Street, featured houses built by the more prosperous citizens. Curiously enough, lawyers and judges lived on Park Street, merchants on Ridge Street, and doctors on High Street.

1910 marked the end of professional used of the Levy Opera House on Court Square, where Jenny Lind had sung and Charlottesville's first telephone had been tested, and where girl and music shows had relieved many "the tired businessmen" of the city.

By 1910 Albemarle County, and more lately Charlottesville, had weathered four wars (fortunately with not too many disastrous effects), the burning and restoration of Thomas Jefferson's Rotunda at the University, and a devastating fire in the East Main Street block between 3rd and 4th Streets. The Monticello Guard, having distinguished itself in the War Between the States, stood ready for a leading role

J. P. Ellington in Charlottesville's first car, 1906

in World War I. By this time the ox, the mule, and the horse were being supplanted in traction power by the Chesapeake and Ohio Railroad and the Southern Railway, by an electric street railway system, and by the electric and gasoline powered automobiles. The picturesque "horse and buggy" days of the earlier era could plainly see the handwriting on the wall. The yielding of the railroads to the motor vehicles would be slower, for the lack of good highways and because, as of 1910, railroad transportation was more economical. Until well after World War I the C. and O.'s "Number Four" and the Southern's "Memphis Special" were enormously popular trains. And at the Union Station Restaurant old William nightly fed a swarm of students with late snacks of sizzling steaks or stacks of batter cakes.

The Charlottesville street railway system had an interesting history. In the late 1880s the cars were pulled by horses and mules, and an additional mule was kept at Vinegar Hill to get the car up that incline. In time the mule was trained on being uncoupled at the top of the hill to return unaided to the bottom to await the next car. Then, in the mid-1890s, the line was electrified and a spur line was run all the way out to Fry's Springs Road to Fry's Springs (there being a passing loop near the old Horse Show Grounds). In earlier days a summer resort hotel had occupied the hill above the springs (one of which had lithia water and one had "pure" water). After fire destroyed the hotel in 1910 the street railway company sponsored the creation of a dance pavilion at the end of this line. Later on, Russell Dettor operated the pavilion until modern times. The Main Street line had a loop at the C. and O. Station and another where the George Rogers Clark Monument now stands just east of the C. and O. bridge over Main Street, then opposite Johnson's Confectionery. Around 1912 the line was extended west on Main Street and north on Rugby Road to a turn-around just south of the Rugby Road bridge. The electric railway line lasted until 1935. Bayard Maupin was the best known motorman and "Fatty" Childress was the veteran conductor.

A close look at this community at this period just before World War I shows a stable, well-balanced rather contented and happy group of people. The residents were largely descendants of the early settlers, and the only sizable minority group was the black population of about 20 percent of the whole. In the period since Reconstruction, the blacks had become widely employed in domestic service, in farm work, and in a surprising number of business enterprises of their own. Race relations during the period were friendly and cooperative, though segregation was still the accepted order. People here generally thought of Charlottesville as a town, rather than as a city. The 1910 census gave Charlottesville a population of 6,765 and Albemarle County 29,871. Local government was still personal; nearly everyone knew everyone else. The invasion of wealthy northerners and westerners to the beautiful rolling hills of Albemarle was well under way, but the pace was slow and, by and large, the newcomers were not only content to absorb the culture they found here but they seemed to make a special effort to do so. A few who found that they didn't fit into this environment quietly went back home, or at least elsewhere. Unfortunately in this respect, "invaders" came to the county in large numbers "after the war" and to some extent they have sought to implant the culture of western cities or other points of origin, and this has tended to bring about some social fragmentation. Albemarle County is still a lovely residential area, but with a rapidly increasing population, the "one happy family" days of the pre-World War I period are, of course, gone.

There is a notable contrast in the economic pattern in the community between pre-war and post-war conditions. In 1910 there were only a handful of industries: the

Building sidewalk downtown, circa 1917

Charlottesville Woolen Mills, the Michie Company, the Charlottesville and the Barnes lumber companies, a few grain mills, and several fruit packing plants. Fruit growing was a big operation in Albemarle County. Crozet was the peach-growing capital of the state. Even the Albemarle Pippin was grown commercially. Because farm labor became scarcer and scarcer, owing to a migration of farm workers to industrial plants, where higher wages (and higher expenses) became a factor, a significant change came over Albemarle agriculture after the war. The largest shift was from fruit growing and marketing to beef cattle.

The four chief sources of wealth in Albemarle County have been for many years agriculture, industry, education and tourism. Before World War I, agriculture was number one in this group, some point after the war agriculture became number four in importance. Naturally this changed the social and economic life of the county in many ways.

The growth of the University of Virginia in the post-war years has been prodigious. It is now a great more like an Ivy League university. The total regular session enrollment in 1910 was less than 1500. The students in various departments—law, medicine, engineering, etc.—knew each other, and men from all departments participated in University athletics and in the social life of the institution. Not having available "wheels," the students remained at the University over weekends and profited from exchanging ideas with each other. President Edwin Anderson Alderman, the first president, was inaugurated in 1904. The Honor System then covered a wider field than now, notably with respect to the dances in the University gymnasium. Attendance at a dance by a student meant that he had had nothing alcoholic to drink since noon of that day. Most of the University dances were formal affairs, with cards made out for the ladies, so that they could meet many of the leading men of the student body. There were no female students then, even in the graduate schools. Driving your girl about during Easter Week in a horse and buggy rented from a local livery stable—Davids and Wood, Irving-Way-Hill, or A. D. Payne's—was a recognized way of calling attention to the loveliness of your date. Even so, measured by accepted standards, the University stood comparatively about as high among American universities as it stands now. Its faculty from 1910 to 1915 included such scholars as John W. Wallet, Francis P. Dunnington and R. M. Bird in Chemistry, Richard Heath Dabney in History, Albert Lefevre in Philosophy, Francis H. Smith and L. G. Hoxton in Physics, Ormond Stone and Samuel A. Mitchell in Astronomy, William H. Echols and James Morris Page in Mathematics, Thomas Walker Page in Economics, Charles W. Kent and C. Alphonso Smith in English Literature, Richard H. Wilson in French, William Harrison Faulkner in German, Milton Humphreys and Robert H. Webb in Greek, Thomas Fitzhugh in Latin, Albert H. Forrest in Biblical History and Literature, Thomas L. Watson in Geology, W. H. Heck and Bruce R. Payne in Education, William Minor Lile, Raleigh C. Minor, Charles A. Graves and Armistead M. Dobie in Law, Richard H. Whitehead, Stephen H. Watts, and J. C. Flippin in Medicine, William M. Thornton, John Lloyd Newcomb and Walter S. Rodman in Engineering and William A. Lambeth and Henry H. Lannigan in Physical Training. This list would appear to be the whole faculty, but it only contains nationally known teachers.

And in 1915, had not the University's football team, made up of Rhodes Scholars to be and practically no substitutes, humbled a great Yale University team, 10 to 0, at New Haven!

Charlottesville has always been an educational center. Some of the many small preparatory schools in earlier years achieved more than local eminence. For example, Pantops Academy, Col. John Bowie Strange's Military Academy,

Bringing in the Hay, 1915

Horace Jones' University School, the Edge Hill School for Girls, the Albemarle Female Institute (later Rawlings Institute), are a few of the well known ones. In 1910 the leading private boys school was the Jefferson School for Boys, conducted by Dr. E. Reinhold Rogers. St. Anne's School for Girls was the premier girls' school. Midway School, at the top of Vinegar Hill, was the largest of the public schools. Blacks attended the Jefferson Public School.

A gala local summer event around 1910 was the Charlottesville Horse Show held at the Horse Show Grounds, which were located on the east side of Fry's Springs Road just south of the Southern Railway bridge. This would be followed by the Keswick Horse Show at its ring near Keswick. The Virginia circuit of horse shows in those years gave great impetus to horse breeding and horse training in this horse-loving community. Uniformed hunt teams were a feature of these shows. There was great rivalry in those days between Albemarle and Orange Counties, with Julian Morris of Keswick representing Albemarle, and Mrs. Gertrude Rives Potts being the most prominent personality from Orange County. Both, as well as many others, had talented horses, some of them winners in the national and English horse shows. After World War I the Albemarle County Fair Grounds, at the north end of Rugby Road, with county fairs, pony and mule races, took the place of the Horse Show Grounds, but they never achieved the first class showmanship of the earlier annual horse shows.

Space in this introduction does not permit a full listing of all the outstanding business and professional offices in the 1910 period. Dr. Paul B. Barringer, Professor of Medicine, had started the University of Virginia Hospital in 1901, and largely through the financial help of Mr. J. A. Patterson (who built the residence on Carter's Mountain) the Martha Jefferson Hospital had been established in 1903. A few of the leading doctors who come to mind were the University surgeons, Dr. Stephen H. Watts and Dr. William H. Goodwin, and Drs. John Staige Davis and J. Carroll Flippin in the medical sciences. Downtown, Dr. William Randolph had retired, and Drs. Edward B. Magruder, Hugh T. Nelson, Monti L. Rea, W. D. Macon, J. E. Early, and Frank T. Daniel were general practitioners; Drs. H. S. Hedges and Robert C. Compton were the eye and throat specialists; and Drs. J. C. Colvin, O. E. Driscoll, and young Harry L. Smith and Charles Beauchamp were the leading dentists. The "horse doctors" of the period were Dr. Theophilous Wood and Dr. John S. Nicholas. Dr. Roy K. Flannigan was the public health director.

The Charlottesville Bar of this period was a distinguished one. Judge William S. Robertson had already moved up to the Virginia Supreme Court of Appeals, and Thomas S. Martin had gone to the United States Senate, but other leaders remained, including Judge Egbert Watson, Judge R. T. W. Duke, Judge John W. Fishburne, Judge G. B. Sinclair, Daniel Harmon, John S. White, Frank Gilmer, and George Perkins. Also coming along as future leaders of the next era, to name only a dozen of them, were William F. Long, W. Allan Perkins, George E. Walker, Archibald D. Dabney, H. W. Walsh, Charles W. Allen, L. T. Hanckel, Jr., Robert H. Wood, Albert S. Bolling, William O. Fife, and Edward O. McCue. The youngest attorney then practicing and the eldest serving until 1977 was George Gilmer. As the local bar had always produced an orator for public occasions, such as Senator and Ambassador William C. Rives in the late 19th century and Col. Micajah Woods in the early 1900s, so around 1910 Judge Richard Thomas Walker Duke was usually called upon when the occasion and the man had to meet. Once at a garden party at Britain's Buckingham Palace he was introduced while eyebrows were lifted, as Richard Thomas Walker, Duke of Albemarle.

The "Police Justice," as the judge of the lower court in Charlottesville was generally called, was a very colorful per-

IMP Society Parade, 1925

son named Charles D. Shackelford, and the very well known clerks of the Corporation (city) and Circuit (county) Courts shortly after 1910 were, respectively, Charles E. ("Chick") Moran and William L. ("Billy") Maupin. The good preservation of court records of this period is a tribute to the care given to their work by these men.

Businesses in the city in the first quarter of the century were usually identified with the persons of families who operated them. Charlottesville had merchants of high standards and fine public spirit. Three of the leading merchant families were Jewish: the Lettermans, Oberdorfers and Kaufmans. All were genuinely respected and popular. Mose Letterman and four brothers operated the Letterman Department Store at 1st and Main; Phil and Julius Oberdorfer had the largest "ladies-to wear" store at 3rd and Main, and across the street from the latter was a men's clothing store owned by Morty and Sol Kaufman, called M. Kaufman's Sons Co. Miss Lou Zimmerman had a smaller ladies' clothing store on Main near 3rd, and Miss Posey had an even smaller one, largely for hats. The most prominent men's clothing store in town was J. B. and W. H. Wood's in the prime business block of Main Street between 3rd and 4th. The gentlemanly manners of the Wood brothers and the high quality of their merchandise made them the favorite clothiers of the University students and faculty. They boasted of their charge accounts to students and their record of never losing any money promised by a student. Of course, if one could afford the price, then about $50, he could have a suit "tailor made" by T. C. Conlon, whose shop was down near Vinegar Hill. Other "dry goods" stores were B. F. Dickerson's in the aforesaid prime block, the Hawkins Brothers store on the next block going west, and then Robey's, a little further west; and uptown near Union Station J. P. Ellingsworth's Bargain Store. The leading shoe stores were W. J. Keller's in the 400 block and J. N. Waddell's in the 300 block of Main Street. The jewelry, watch repair and optical shops were Keller and George and C. S. Apple.

The H. M. Gleason family had the largest downtown grocery store, on the corner of 4th and Main. Other grocery stores were those of S. J. Robinson and Sons, at 2nd West and Main, and the Midway Market, a few blocks further west on Main Street. One of the Gleasons, Hope Gleason, branched out into a farm supply store, which is now the large establishment of H. M. Gleason & Co., Inc. on Garrett Street.

There was a popular bakery and confectionery shop on the north side of Main between 3rd and 4th operated by J. C. Mathews, and uptown just east of the C. and O. bridge was Johnson's Confectionery, later a favorite eating place for University students. Both had excellent ice creams.

Naturally in a "town" of this size would be some household furnishings and appliance shops. Charlottesville had some excellent ones. Covington and Peyton had a very high class china and glass shop, John A. Gilmore a fine furniture store, and J. M. Perley and M. C. Thomas, all on Main Street downtown, had both furniture and other house furnishings. Perley had, in addition, an undertaking department for funerals, and M. C. Thomas had a large business in renting out furniture for University student rooms. Electric supplies came from the Sensibaugh-Ritchie electric appliances store. Walter Page's father-in-law had the first florist shop, King Greenhouses, at the corner of 14th St. and West Main (then called University Avenue). Walter Page continued it as Page Greenhouses. The downtown drug stores were Brown's at 5th and Main, Timberlake's near its present site, Pence and Sterling's on the southwest corner of East 2nd and Main, and Miller's on Main near West 2nd. Uptown, and vying for the University trade, were the S. C. Chancellor and W. H. Sheppe (called the University Drug Store) drug stores at the Corner. Anderson Brothers Book Store, the University Book Store, the University Grocery, John S. LaRowe's Pool Room,

Salvation Army Outing, 1914

and Charlie Brown's Barber Shop were other thriving businesses at the Corner.

As the center of the farming area, Charlottesville had the stores that supported an agricultural economy. R. F. Harris and Company, half-way uptown on the north side of Main Street, sold carriages, wagons, harnesses and plows, and had as an adjunct enterprise an iron foundry. Irving-Way-Hall, at the east end of town sold carriages and also had livery stable and undertaking services. Goodyear and Robertson had the leading saddlery shop, located on 4th Street, between Main and Market. There were two hardware stores, the Charlottesville Hardware Company in the "prime" block, and on the other side of Main Street, W. T. Martin's Hardware, J. B. Andrew's, at the foot of Vinegar Hill, was the feed store for farm animals. Wood and West, near the C. and O. Station, and Burnley Coal Company, near the Union Station, supplied the community's coal, and the Charlottesville Lumber Company and Barnes Lumber Company, both at the east end of town, met the building construction needs.

The Peoples National Bank (formerly located where Timberlake's Drug Store is now) and the Farmers and Merchant Bank, the Virginia State Building and Loan Company, and the Peoples Mortgage Corporation helped to build the expanding town into a city.

It must be confessed that the listing of all these business establishments from memory may have shown errors in location and in the initials in names, but the surnames in general are correct. It is only to be hoped that the names of some of the places, persons, and things here mentioned will give a little more life-likeness to Mr. Rufus W. Holsinger's art.

Bernard P. Chamberlain
July 1976

HOLSINGER'S CHARLOTTESVILLE

"Both the natural beauty of the surrounding countryside and the man made beauty of Charlottesville combine to weave a tapestry of American history of which few other towns or cities can boast."

— JOHN F. KENNEDY
President of the United States

Holsinger Studio

❦ HOLSINGER STUDIO ❦

Rufus W. "Holly" Holsinger would never have been a photographer had it not been for a mistake which occurred while he was living in his native state of Pennsylvania. At the time he was teaching in the Pleasantville Normal School, he developed a cough which was incorrectly diagnosed as consumption (tuberculosis). The only prescription for the disease was that he get plenty of fresh air and sunshine. In following this advice, he decided to turn photography, then a summer hobby, into a profit-making profession. He began by traveling in a horse-drawn cart from town to town taking graduation pictures at local schools. At this peak he traveled through most of the east coast pursuing his profession. However, sometime during the late 1880s he passed through Charlottesville, liked the town, and decided to stay. One reason for his decision was increased competition from speculative firms which were beginning to enter the photography business, particularly in the high volume area of graduation pictures.

What exact year Holsinger moved to Charlottesville is not known. However, it is known from receipts of purchase still in existence that he bought City Studio in 1887 and Wampler's in 1889. From that time until 1925 he photographed and preserved the people, places and events of the Charlottesville area. By profession, Holsinger was primarily a portrait photographer. Some eighty percent of the surviving negatives are of his portrait customers. According to his son, Ralph Holsinger, he photographed many notables, including Robert E. Lee. Unfortunately, many valuable negatives were lost in a 1910 studio fire.

Of greater significance are the approximately two thousand negatives of significant events—building dedications, business openings, sporting events, etc.—and people busily engaged in the routines of their daily lives over a forty-year period. Many of these photographs were just part of his business. For example, during the height of his reputation, Holsinger was the official photographer for six different railroads and traveled great distances to photograph train wrecks. He was also chosen to make the photograph of Monticello that appeared on the original two-dollar bill.

Aside from business, a great deal of Holsinger's work was done for pleasure. Pictures of prim women on street corners and gnarled old men in ox carts would hardly have been subjects for a profit-seeking business. It is also probable that motives other than profit caused him to photograph such historic events as the burning of the Rotunda at the University of Virginia.

Regardless of the exact reasons behind Holsinger's photographs, one thing is certain: it took a considerable amount of effort and expertise to make them. Today, our technology has made it possible for anyone to take a photograph of a reasonable quality with very little effort and practically no knowledge of the photographic process. Such was not the case in the day of Rufus Holsinger. He entered the field of photography when it was in its infancy. It was 1839 when Louis Daguerre developed the first practical process for forming a photographic image, and Holsinger made his first Charlottesville photographs about fifty years later. The method by which Holsinger made most of his photographs was an extremely cumbersome process known as the wet plate method. He began with an ordinary plate of glass usually eight to ten inches in size, although the size varied from as small as five by seven inches to as large as fourteen by seventeen inches. Under conditions of extremely low light illumination, he spread onto the plate a mixture containing

Camera used by Rufus W. "Holly" Holsinger

potassium iodide called "collodion." After this, he dipped the plate into a solution of one part silver nitrate to twelve parts water. The plate stayed in this solution for approximately six to eight minutes after which it was placed into a light tight negative carrier. Then while the negative was still wet, the plate was put into the camera and the negative exposed. This process had to be repeated each time a photograph was to be made, for once the collodion solution dried, the negative could no longer be used.

Once the wet plate had been made, a new challenge awaited him when he actually took the picture. To begin with, the bulkiness of a camera that could accommodate an eight by ten inch negative was considerable, and the system by which the subject was viewed was confusing, for the image that was seen through the lens of the camera was upside-down and backwards.

Despite the many obstacles which faced Holsinger and his fellow photographers, their photographs are some of the most beautiful ever made. The quality of these old photographs is partly due to the inherent qualities of the wet plate negative which was known for its unusual softness in tones of gray and almost grainless clarity. In addition to this, the extremely large negative size allowed a print with a degree of sharpness seldom seen today.

Aside from the techniques mastered by Holsinger, his artistic treatment of his subjects is admirable. In both his portraits and his more historic renditions of Charlottesville, he exercised a fluidity of posing and overall composition which allow his photographs to be both dynamic and universal in their appeal. When this factor is added to Holsinger's technical expertise and ability to manipulate his negatives in the darkroom to achieve the best possible effect, it is easy to appreciate the Holsinger Collection in a more complex way.

One story which does much to round out the existence of Rufus Holsinger as a turn of the century photographer concerns the burning of the Rotunda. Holsinger was attending church on that Sunday morning in 1895 when the fire was discovered. Upon hearing the news, he rushed to his cart and drove immediately to his studio. Once there, he loaded up his camera, prepared his negatives, and got to the fire in time to photograph the Rotunda just before the dome fell through. One must attribute this accomplishment, at least in part, to Holsinger's speedy thoroughbred horse who was reputed to be so fast that Holsinger had to put wire wheels on his cart because the horse traveled at such speeds that wooden spokes would shatter. Later on, Holsinger became one of the first citizens of Charlottesville to own an electric car.

Holsinger practiced his well-mastered craft into the twentieth century though he suffered from repeated ill-health. In 1925, as he was recovering from a serious operation, he had a fainting spell and fell from the second story window of his studio. Although a telephone wire broke his fall, he suffered a fractured skull and was unable to continue his profession. From that time until 1969, his son, Ralph Holsinger, whom he had trained since childhood, took over the operation of the studio. The younger Holsinger proved to be a skillful photographer in his own right, and his artistic photographs provide as valuable a record of life in Charlottesville during the middle years of the twentieth century as his father's photographs of an earlier period.

At hand is a selected collection of the photographs of Rufus Holsinger, who has provided us with a rare opportunity to see how Charlottesville and its citizens looked and lived more than a half century ago.

Barbara Rushia
Manager, Holsinger Studio
1976

Monticello

Monticello was the love of Thomas Jefferson's life. He began construction in 1768, and did not finish until 1809. This internationally acclaimed architectural masterpiece designed by the ingenious Mr. Jefferson was largely built by slaves under Jefferson's careful supervision. Most of the building materials were prepared on the place. After Jefferson's death in 1826 the house was sold. In 1830 it was bought by J. T. Barclay, who sold it six years later to Commodore Uriah P. Levy. Except for the period of The War when Monticello was confiscated by the Confederate Government, it remained in the Levy family until its purchase by the Monticello Foundation in 1923. Note the lack of railings on the long terraces, which left the chambers at each end in stark simplicity.

Michie Tavern

Michie's Tavern was originally located on The Old Buck Mountain Road near Earlysville, on land patented in 1735 by Major John Henry, the father of the famous orator, Patrick Henry. In 1746 he sold the land, unimproved, to "Scotch John" Michie. To accommodate the many travelers seeking food and shelter, his son William opened his home as an "Ordinary" in 1784. The tavern prospered, and was owned and operated by descendants for well over a century. By the 1920s the old colonial tavern was no longer needed to serve the functions of its past. It was purchased in 1927 by Mrs. Markwood Henderson who had it dismantled piece by piece and carefully reconstructed at its present site on Monticello Mountain to house her collection of antiques. It is now known as Historic Michie Tavern.

Pantops Academy

Pantops Academy was a Presbyterian school for boys located east of Charlottesville. It was opened in 1879 by Rev. Edgar Woods and served as a preparatory school for the University of Virginia. The chief demand made of every pupil was "that he conduct himself as a gentleman". Students were required to attend church on Sunday mornings and to join the principal and his family in Bible readings in the evenings. The school had a high reputation and attracted pupils from twenty-eight states and several foreign countries. The campus consisted of three large buildings, providing living quarters, classrooms, a central hall and a gymnasium. The Academy was at the height of its prosperity when, in 1905, the principal, John P. Sampson suddenly closed the school for "reasons connected with my family".

Charlottesville Woolen Mills

Founded in 1830, the Charlottesville Woolen Mills, located at the end of East Market Street, manufactured cheap cloth for slaves and later, uniforms for the Confederacy. The success of the mill after The War was due to Henry Clay Marchant, who guided the business through the Reconstruction period and several severe recessions. The mill was one of the area's largest employers, and many employees lived in houses built by the Mills. By 1900 it had a national reputation, and supplied uniforms for most of the nation's military schools, including West Point. Many municipal employees across the U. S. also wore Charlottesville fabrics, as did most railroad crewmen. However, the mill could not modernize and closed in the early 1960s. Many of the original buildings have since been razed.

Charlottesville and Albemarle Power Plant

A new electric-generating plant was built on the Rivanna River in 1914, the year of this photograph. This new plant replaced the old one located behind the C & O yard between 5th and 7th Streets, and had a capacity of 1500 kilowatts. Before the new plant was built, electrical service in Charlottesville was severely limited. Now, service was extended into most residential areas in the city. Rural service remained virtually non-existent with the exception of a few privately built lines. A decade later a transmission line from a power plant in West Virginia was connected into the city and the C & A plant's importance declined. After a power station was built at Bremo Bluff in 1931 the plant was used very little, although it was briefly revived during WW II. It was abandoned altogether after the war and sold.

Building Free Bridge Road

This 1917 photograph shows the building of the first paved road in Charlottesville (now East High Street). The camera looks east to an early version of Free Bridge. Unlike today, bridges were built at the most convenient spot on the river and the roads led up to them along the banks. Note the long sweep of the road along the river. The technology of the time made road building a slow, difficult process. The road bed was graded and forms were built to hold the concrete. The concrete mixer in the picture was a fairly recent invention. Stones and cement were loaded on a lift (not shown). Steam power raised the lift, pouring the materials into the mixing drum. The concrete was then poured into the forms. One workman is shown smoothing the wet concrete while the bed is prepared for the next section.

Colonial Hotel

This 1915 photograph shows the Colonial Hotel, formerly an annex of the Monticello Hotel on Court Square. The building date of the original tavern on this site is uncertain, but it was sometime before 1791. From that time on it was the site of public entertainment. The first tavern was a wooden, two and a half story building called the "Eagle". There was a deep porch along the front of it on which traveling peddlers sold their wares. Later the wooden structure was replaced by the present low brick building. In 1869 the tavern changed hands and became the Farish Hotel. Before World War I the tavern changed hands again and was named the Colonial Hotel. During Prohibition the hotel felt it necessary to assure its customers with a sign stating: "Colonial Hotel *Still* In Business."

McKee Block

Pictured above is the Court Square area before 1915. Dating back to colonial times, this little street was known as McKee block, named for Dr. McKee who lived in the first house in the row. These buildings comprised the central part of the town in the early 1800s. Other residents on the block included a hatter, a tailor, a printer, and various merchants and grocers. The third building in the row was once the Central Hotel. This building was moved to McKee block from Milton, once a thriving town on the Rivanna River. Several houses were moved from Milton when the town declined after the coming of the railroad in the 1840s. McKee block faced east towards the Court House between High Street (Maiden Lane) and Jefferson Street. The block was razed before 1921 to make way for Jackson Park.

Albemarle County Court House

In 1761 the seat of Albemarle County was moved to Charlottesville from Scottsville. A court house was erected near the site of the left wing of the present structure. Court Square was enclosed by a railing in 1792, when the pillory, stocks and whipping post were already in place and in use. In 1803 the north, or rear wing of the present building was built. This wing, called the "Common Temple" by Thomas Jefferson, also served as a church. The front section of the Court House was built in 1860, and the portico was added in the early 1870s. This photograph was taken a year after the Monument to the Confederate Soldiers with cannon on either side of it was unveiled in 1909. In 1938 the Court House was completely restored. Yellow paint was removed to expose the red brick.

St. Anne's School

St. Anne's School was operated in this building at the corner of East Jefferson and 10th Streets. It was founded in 1857 as the Albemarle Female Institute, and in 1897 became the Rawlings Institute. An early school catalogue advertised the school as "the peer of any in the land". The Rawlings Institute closed in 1909, but a year later Henry Bettinger Lee reopened the school as St. Anne's, an Episcopal Church School for Girls. In 1924 the school established an "outdoor school" campaign which emphasized athletics. A West Point officer was hired to drill the girls in exercise and posture. In 1939 St. Anne's moved to its present location on Ivy Road. In recent years it merged with Belfield School. The building pictured here became an apartment house. It was later torn down to make way for doctors' offices.

Monticello Hotel

On the site of the old Eagle Tavern which dated back to 1791, construction of the Monticello Hotel was begun in 1925. Located on the South side of Public Square or Court Square as we now call it, the new hotel offered modern conveniences and featured an extremely popular dining room. Because of its distance from the railway station, a hack was hired to meet each train, give visitors help with their luggage, and take them to the hotel. In 1927 the Thomas Jefferson Beacon, one of the most powerful searchlights in the world, was installed atop the hotel. The beacon could be seen for a distance of 200 miles, and occasionally was trained on Monticello at night. In the early 1940s the captain of a zeppelin that made an appearance in Charlottesville reported that the beam of the searchlight kept the interior of the ship's cabin well lighted all the way back to Langley Field, Hampton, Va. In the early 1970s the hotel was renovated into condominium apartments.

Lee Park

Lee Park is located off Jefferson Street, between 1st and 2nd Streets. The site was formerly the home of Valentine Southall and, in later years, Mrs. Charles Venable. In 1924 a statute of Robert E. Lee on his famous steed, Traveller, was added to the park. At the time this photograph was taken the base of the monument was already in place. Also, two large millstones were placed in the park. These stones were said to have come from the original mill of Peter Jefferson, Thomas Jefferson's father, which was located in Shadwell. The park and monument were the gifts of Charlottesville's great benefactor, Paul Goodlow McIntire. The building with the tall columns was the public library. Notice, in the background, how close the countryside was to the city at this time.

Main Street

This 1922 photograph looks west on Main Street; Vinegar Hill curves off to the left. Before the street was laid in brick, there were only stepping stones to help pedestrians avoid slogging through the dirt and mud of this well traveled road. When first laid, the bricks in the street had soft green, pink and blue hues, and after a rain they glistened with color. The streetcar tracks ran down the middle of the street, and every so often there was a double set of tracks so that trolleys going in opposite directions could pass. Many of the buildings pictured here are still standing, although the first floor facades have changed over the years. Much of the flavor of this period of Charlottesville is still retained in the upper story facades which remain virtually unchanged since the turn of the century.

Salvation Army

Captain Paul Jones began the work of the Salvation Army in Charlottesville in 1912. The first Citadel was at 287 W. Main Street. The Salvation Army headquarters were moved several times over the next few years, and for a brief time were located at 411 W. Main Street where this photograph was taken. The event recorded here is Thanksgiving Dinner, November 30, 1916. Present at the dinner were children from the Sunday school, members of the Ladies Home League, and other persons who attended the non-denominational Salvation Army services. Standing before the table (left) are a group of local businessmen who served on the advisory board of the organization. They included Messrs. Adams, Clayton, Irving, and Thomas. The Salvation Army moved from this building in 1917.

Peoples National Bank

In 1916 construction of the Peoples National Bank building was underway on East Main Street. Until the building was completed, Peoples was located further up the block (notice the sign with the clock), where Timberlake's Drug Store is now located. During the prosperous 1920s, Peoples was instrumental in the growth of business in the city. It survived the Depression, and went on to become the seventh largest bank in Virginia. In 1963 Peoples merged with a Norfolk bank to form the Virginia National Bank. Pictured are some of the leading businesses at that time: Waddell's shoe store, Wood's clothing store, Tilman's department store, and the Charlottesville Hardware Store. Part of this block was gutted by a disastrous fire in 1905 but was quickly rebuilt.

Timberlake's Drug Store

Pictured here is the interior of Timberlake's Drug Store shortly after it opened in 1917. Previously, the building was occupied by Peoples National Bank. In those days Timberlake's sold not only prescription drugs, cosmetics, etc., but also house paints and garden supplies. The paints were hand-mixed on the spot in the store. The fountain sold sodas, ice cream, coffee and tea. A common order was "give me a dope", meaning, of course, "give me a Coke". In 1960 the building was completely renovated, including changing the facade back to its pre-1905 (the year of a major fire) look. Today the massive counters and shelves are gone, along with the old fashioned marble-top tables and wrought iron chairs, which were considered obsolete. The fountain, which was located near the entrance, is now in the back of the store. The original tile floor, however, is still intact.

Waddell's Shoe Store

Waddell's Shoe Store was established in 1895 by M. C. Thomas and J. N. Waddell. When this photograph was taken (1916) it, along with Keller's, was the leading shoe store in Charlottesville. Waddell's was located in the prime business block between 3rd and 4th streets, next to Peoples National Bank and Wood's clothing store. It is believed the men in this photograph are Mr. Waddell, Mr. Shackelford, Mr. Barksdale and Mr. Lee. For many years Waddell's did a thriving business, dealing in luggage and hosiery as well as shoes. During this era fashions were stable, and the same shoe styles remained popular year after year. However, after World War II clothing fads began to take their toll on small stores like Waddell's, who found it impossible to keep all the various styles in stock and were forced out of business.

Lafayette Theater

Charlottesville has always managed to have an entertainment hall of one sort or another. In the early 1800s it was the Town Hall across from the Court House. Later in the century, Jefferson Monroe Levy bought the hall and renovated it as an opera house; however, it was small, cramped and dark. In 1896 Jacob Letterman built the Jefferson Auditorium, which was a great improvement over the Levy Opera House. The Auditorium featured first class theater and opera, but unfortunately the hall burned in 1907. Seating 1,000, the Lafayette Theater (pictured) was principally a movie house with an almost daily change of features—the cost of which was a modest 10–30 cents. Elegant in decor, the Lafayette was graced with a $15,000 pipe organ that was played, usually extemporaneously, as a mood-setting compliment to silent movies.

Co-Operative Drug Company

The Co-Operative Drug Company was one of the early "chain" stores in the years before WWI. The profit sharing mentioned in the sign was in the form of a rebate given to customers who spent over a certain amount of money in a year. After taking over the building from the City Confectionery Company, the new tenants set about remodeling. They bricked up the windows facing the side street and put a large white facade on the front of the building. Large vessels of colored water (one red, one green) were hung from each window. The interior had tile floors, a soda fountain, and two slow-moving fans. After several years the store closed and the building was occupied by the Standard Drug Company. Later it was the home of a music store. The building was on the corner of 3rd and Main St.

McGuffey School

Built in 1916, McGuffey School served the city's grammar school children for over fifty years. It was named after the famous educator, William Holmes McGuffey, who came to Charlottesville in 1845 as Professor of Moral Philosophy at the University. McGuffey is best known as the author of a series of readers, spellers and primers. His books, which are still popular, were the first of their type. They appealed to children on their own level, and children found them more enjoyable than the Puritan-inspired readers of the early 1800s. A distinctive feature of the readers was the use of illustrations. The man in the foreground of this photograph is Dr. James G. Johnson, Superintendent of Schools. The building, located on 2nd Street, N.W., is now a city-owned art center.

Charlottesville Lumber Company

The Charlottesville Lumber Company was begun as a saw mill in 1893 by L. W. Graves. In the early 1900s the company sold rough and dressed lumber and other building materials. It also served as a general contractor, building many homes in Charlottesville, and featured a custom mill works plant. Lumbering was no easy job at the time. Once the trees were felled, the sawlogs were hauled to the mill in horse-drawn wagons over muddy roads. Often this was an all-day adventure. Although this building has undergone extensive remodeling since this 1917 photograph was taken, it still stands on the corner of Avon and Garrett Streets, next to the C. & O. railroad. Notice the shadow of the Belmont Bridge to the left.

Charlottesville Ice Company

This 1915 photograph shows all the services offered by the Charlottesville Ice Company. Besides selling ice, the company sold ice cream, beef and pork. In the abbatoir animals were slaughtered and dressed, and chitlins, scrapple and lard were made. The stables housed the horses that pulled the ice wagons. The company was established in 1890 by John Frank Elliot. In 1914 his twin sons took over the business and eventually changed the name to Elliot's Ice Company. In 1959 the company was bought by the Monticello Dairy and moved to Grady Avenue. Notice the conveyor belt that carried ice to produce-laden train cars. Near the company's offices was the site of Margurita's famous brothel. Much of this area was razed by the city in 1973 as part of a redevelopment project.

H. H. Hankins Hay and Grain

Henley Hutchinson Hankins established this business just before 1900. He dealt in hay, straw, grain, dairy feed, fertilizers, poultry supplies and sugar. Hay was shipped in from as far away as Canada and New York state. As many as nine boxcar loads of hay would arrive in the morning and be sold by night. Hankins also sold sugar by the boxcar load, a practice which attracted a good deal of attention from law enforcement officials during the Prohibition era. When the circus came to Charlottesville, Hankins loaded wagons with grain, hay and straw and drove to the fairgrounds, then located just across from the Charlottesville Lumber Company near the Belmont Bridge. This picture shows sacks of grain that have just been loaded from the chute into the wagon. Mr. Hankins is standing under the window.

Brown Milling Company

In the days of this 1917 photograph, Brown Milling Company, like many other mills, not only processed grains, but did a lively business of exchange as well. Rough grains were brought here from the surrounding countryside and even from other states. Farmers drove large horse-drawn wagons loaded with wheat, corn, oats and rye, to the mill for a morning of selling and trading. It was common for a man to exchange a quantity of unmilled grains for a proportional quantity of flour. Brown's advertisements of the time appealed, in no uncertain terms, to local chauvinism. An ad for Monticello Pride Flour asked rhetorically, "What would our merchants do if everybody bought their goods in another city? It would kill the town! Spend your money with our people."

Down in the Bottom

Mr. Lionnie Vest, born in one of the houses pictured, remembers this area referred to as "down in the bottom" because of the creek that ran through the area. Here is how Garrett Street looked in 1915. The fourth house in the row, a large white clapboard, belonged to Matt Thompson, proprietor of a brothel. The best known employee was Margurita, who later opened Charlottesville's most famous house of ill repute on the next block. According to one long-time resident, the "lucky bean tree" on the corner was the site of local crap games. The sign on the tree reads: "Base-ball Tonight—Colored Jefferson vs. T.S.T.—Today—Horse Show Grounds". This photograph shows that many roads in the city were not in much better shape than the country roads. In the background the smoke stacks of the Charlottesville Ice Company are visible.

The Monticello Guard...

The Monticello Guard was formed in 1857 and was descended from other military units which had served Charlottesville from as early as 1758. One early unit was the Gentlemen Volunteers of Albemarle which served under the command of Gen. Lafayette during the Revolutionary War. The company fought bravely in several actions during the Civil War and took part in Pickett's Charge at Gettysburg. In 1916 the Guard was sent to Texas to help guard the Mexican border against Pancho Villa. Shortly thereafter, the company was mustered into service and sent to France. After WWI the unit was reactivated as Company K and became part of the National Guard. The men of Company K were called to arms in WWII and again distinguished themselves in battle.

Marching Off to War

This photograph and the one on the preceding page show the Monticello Guard parading down Main Street on their way to Camp McClellan, Alabama for training in trench warfare. Of that September afternoon in 1917, *The Daily Progress* wrote: "The slanting rays of the setting sun were even then casting long shadows athwart the scene, and as the last gleams lit up the manly faces of the khaki-clad boys getting ready to go in their turn if need be at the call of duty, the heart leapt up in awe and admiration at the quiet display of the Nation's might and oneness." The company served in the Meuse-Argonne and Chateau-Thierry sectors of France for most of the war. It suffered heavy casualties in both dead and wounded. Several Medal of Honor winners have served in the Monticello Guard.

On November 11, 1918 the Armistice ending the Great War was signed. The world rejoiced with the news and Charlottesville was no exception. The Daily Progress *reported the following:*

The people of this city and surrounding country united on yesterday afternoon in a monster mass meeting at and around the Midway School Building in commemoration of the great news that stirred the town early in the day, of the final submission of the despicable Huns to the armistice terms handed them last Friday by Generalissimo Ferdinand Foch and the outpouring and exercises were perhaps the most impressive and spontaneous of any ever held here at any previous period of the community's history.

After the whole town and county had turned the forenoon into a general holiday making, in which young and old combined in enthusiastic jollification to show their pride, relief and joy at the signal victory of Allied and American arms in the mighty conflict brought on by Germany, the people assembled en masse at the call of Major E. G. Haden and many leading citizens in every walk and sphere of life, and listened to patriotic addresses and grateful prayers by eloquent and forceful speakers, whose words voiced the deep and lasting gratitude of a loyal people to the God of Battles who gave the victory, and interpreted the sentiments of the public in the glad hour of the world war's cessation of mortal strife.

It was both impressive and pregnant with vital meaning, and the spontaneous outpouring was the reflex of the deep-seated patriotism and unswerving determination that have marked this historic section's attitude since the fateful day in April 1917, when the Nation was called to arms by the President and Congress of the United States. All classes were present, and young and old vied with each other in making the celebration epochal and whole souled and in going on record in perpetuating unbounded admiration and love for the heroic sons of America whose self-sacrificing devotion to duty had made the success of the cause swift and sure.

After the city had given itself up to jollification and enthusiasm in every form all during the morning hours, during which all places of business were closed in honor of the event and every form of noise was indulged in to the fullest that the ingenuity of the young people and the sturdy sons of labor at factories and on the railroads could devise, the holiday crowd packed the business portion of Main Street like a circus day, awaiting the parade.

At the Midway School the ample mound was literally covered with people, every available inch being occupied around the two sides facing north and west, and the streets near by being packed to the limit with men, women and children, who never ceased giving vent to their enthusiasm in cheers and every form of making the welkin ring.

The formal exercises were simple, brief and impressive, as suited the occasion; but the speakers showed they had caught the significance and epochal meaning of the times, and voiced the throbbing feeling of gratitude and elation at the victory won against such a dangerous and malignant foe. Mayor Haden first called on Dr. Henry B. Lee of the Episcopal Church, to offer up the invocation, and this cultured and deeply spiritual divine fittingly expressed the sentiments of the assemblage in an eloquent and moving prayer of thanks and praise to Almighty God for his heavenly care and protection.

Next the Mayor introduced Rev. Henry W. Battle, the spiritual minded, patriotic and eloquent pastor of the Baptist denomination, and he made a most impassioned and moving address that stirred his hearers to enthusiasm and applause.

He paid his respects to the prime author of all the horrid deeds that have marked this conflict as the most despicable that ever blotted history's pages and raised a storm of applause as he expressed his joy in the final overthrow of the Kaiser, "the Beast of Berlin".

Peace Celebration November 11, 1918

Midway Building

The Midway Building, located at the junction of Main and Ridge Streets, was built in 1828. It was intended to be leased as a hotel to serve visiting families of University students. The original house was 50 feet by 55 feet, and had a huge dining room, stables, kitchen, smoke house and large yard. During the Civil War, it served as a hospital for sick and wounded soldiers. Later, in the 1880s, it housed one of the finest private preparatory schools for boys. It later became a public secondary school called the Midway School. Another building was added in the rear as expansion for a high school became necessary. Before being torn down, the building housed various public agencies, including the Health Department and City Court. This 1917 photograph was taken before the Lewis and Clark monument was installed on West Main Street.

West Main Street

This 1917 photograph was taken at the top of Vinegar Hill, looking west. Much of this scene has been demolished by the city for redevelopment, but a few buildings pictured here still remain. One survivor is Inge's Market at 4th Street (once called "Bull Alley"). The building was erected in the early 1800s on what had been a farm. The store was established in 1891 and has changed hands only once, from founder to son until recently. Vinegar Hill itself (once called Random Row) was filled with shops and homes, all long gone. The origin of Vinegar Hill's name is a matter of debate. Some claim it was named after Vinegar Hill in Eniscorthy, Ireland, the site of fighting between Protestants and Catholics nearly 200 years ago. Others say it derived from the illicit trade of whiskey once carried out by grocers on the hill.

Charlottesville & Albemarle Railway Offices

The C. & A. Ry. not only operated the town's streetcar line, but it owned the power plant, and also sold electrical appliances. The ranges on the truck were the first in Charlottesville and were installed in the Wertenbaker Apartments still located on University Circle now under a different name. The utility sold appliances to encourage people to use more electricity. The truck in the picture ran on batteries which were charged every night. It remained in use until 1925. The offices here at the corner of Ridge and Main Streets served as the company's headquarters until 1958, well after it had merged with VEPCO. The driver of the truck, Emmett Dudley, was a line foreman. The man in the white suit was the superintendent, Kirby Snyder. The other person was Claudie Dudley, a "utility man."

Gleason Hotel

Built in 1890 by Michael S. Gleason, this was the largest continuously operating hotel in Charlottesville until the coming of the Monticello Hotel. The kitchen did a thriving business, despite the lack of refrigeration. Breakfast and dinners were served, and there was a separate tea room. Traveling salesman of the day agreed that there was no finer place to dine, and the deep porch with its rocking chairs lured many a tired soul. This 1915 photograph shows the hotel in its heyday. A good part of its business came from the passengers travelling on the Southern Railway, and as the popularity of train transportation dropped, so did the businesses in the train station neighborhood. In 1935 the hotel changed hands and became the Albemarle Hotel. The building is now occupied by Quest Book Store, with various offices on the floors above.

American Railway Express

The American Express company entered the freight business in 1850 and gradually expanded its operation to include other activities, most notably money orders and travel. When the parcel post service was begun in 1913, the company lost a great deal of its domestic freight service, but countered by expanding its foreign freight business. With the coming of the First World War, the government caused the major freight shippers to merge into an entity known as the American Railway Express, as part of the war effort. Very simply, goods were shipped by train and then delivered from the station to wagons, like the one pictured here. The express office at the Union Station is shown elsewhere. The man wearing the cap has been identified as George Robertson. The other man is a company official.

Fresh To Your Grocery Counter

The foundation of the Nabisco empire was the invention of the wax paper wrapper, the "inner seal," which allowed crackers to arrive fresh from big-city bakeries. They were shipped by rail and then delivered by wagons, like the one here, to stores. The smartly-groomed horses and neat wagon were typical of the company which warned its drivers: "An unfavorable impression is left in the minds of the public when wagons are not painted, horses are not properly groomed and harnesses not in the best condition." In 1915 Nabisco claimed all their wagons lined up would stretch for four miles. But the days of the horse-drawn wagon were numbered. In 1914, after a brief experience with electric trucks, gasoline trucks were introduced. By 1923 Nabisco's entire delivery fleet was gasoline powered.

From the Country

Ox power was not uncommon in Charlottesville, as this March 1913 photograph shows. All county roads were unpaved, and the rains of spring quickly turned them into quagmires, as the mud-caked cart wheels will attest. Some people claim that oxen were the most dependable draft animals. Horses, it was said, were unable to pull a wagon through deep mud, and mules were too smart to try. Evidently, the driver here has brought sacks of potatoes to town to sell or trade for merchandise. He is parked in front of a grocery store on West Main Street and, incidentally, in front of the old Holsinger Studio. In the background is the trainmaster's office of the Southern Railway and a trolley car. Main Street, at the time, was still paved in brick. Also, notice the hand-made qualities of the cart.

Queen Charlotte Hotel

In the late 1800s a member of the Peyton family opened her home to the traveling public, offering an exclusive inn. Soon, however, more rooms were needed to meet the demands of the heavily traveled railroads, and the Queen Charlotte Hotel was built on the front lawn of the old house. The hotel, located on West Main Street across from the Southern Railway's Union Station, prospered throughout the early decades of this century until the railroads began to decline. The Queen Charlotte boasted of having the finest food and hospitality in the area. But in the early 1950s when the city adopted a building code, the hotel was doomed. In 1955 the hotel's owners decided to raze the building rather than pay the high costs of renovation and repair. The site occupied by the hotel is now a used car lot.

Southern Railway Station

The 1919 photograph shows a recently completed West Main Street bridge over the Southern Railway tracks which replaced the earlier wooden bridge. Also shown is the passengers' walkway leading from the street into the station building. This walkway led directly into a porch, complete with skylight, on the second floor of the building where there was a popular restaurant which boasted of having the freshest seafood in town—delivered each day by train. This walkway was torn down some fifty years ago. Also, there is a large pile of bricks which was used to build a walkway by the tracks. The operation tower (center background) is long gone, as is the express office (extreme left foreground). The fence along the sidewalk has also been replaced. This photograph was taken from the roof of the old Holsinger Studio.

Southern Railway Wreck

Early in the morning of December 3, 1912, a passenger train collided with a freight train in the lower end of the Southern yards, demolishing three cars loaded with oranges. The fruit was scattered in every direction, causing what *The Daily Progress* described as an "orangeshower." A large number of people turned out to see this spectacular wreck, and "many seemed to forget that the oranges belonged to the railway company and carried off a quantity of fruit." However, this picture has not caught anyone in the act. The engine and one car of the passenger train were derailed, but none of the passengers or crew members of either train were injured. The wreck, which was by no means an uncommon occurrence, was caused by an open switch. By evening the main track was cleared and traffic resumed.

"Wertland"

This 1914 photograph was taken from what is now the corner of 13th and Wertland Street. The nearest house, 1301 Wertland, was built sometime before 1830 by William Wertenbaker, who was selected by Thomas Jefferson to be the University's librarian. The house was later the home of Milton Humphreys, Professor of Greek at the University. Professor Humphreys rented the house for a number of years and finally purchased it in 1891. Students at the time were known to be reluctant to accept invitations to Professor Humphreys' table because his house was "such a distance from the University." At Professor Humphreys' death the house passed to his heirs and is now an office building. The white house has been replaced by an apartment building. Interestingly, artist Georgia O'Keefe lived at Wertland when she was a young woman.

Humane Society

The concern for preventing child abuse and cruelty to animals was among the finer expressions of the Progressive reform movement. These women are shown distributing copies of the 1915 newsletter published by the American Humane Educational Society to passers-by on the West Main Street railway bridge. Local chapters of the American Humane Association usually maintained pet shelters and, on the state level, lobbied for the passage of laws to protect children and animals. A major goal of the movement was to have humane education taught in public schools. Unfortunately, the society had little impact on Virginia lawmakers. As late as 1922 the state had no laws protecting children or animals. It outlawed public fights between men and animals, although cockfights were allowed to continue.

Fry's Springs

Before the establishment of Farmington and the Monticello Hotel, the Fry's Springs dance pavilion was popular for debutante parties, horse shows, and charity balls. The Fry's Springs complex was a famous summer resort. It included the Jefferson Park Hotel (which burned down in 1910), a casino, menagerie, open-air theater, merry-go-round, and other amusements. It is said that the first movies shown in Charlottesville were at Fry's Springs. The resort was owned by the Charlottesville & Albemarle Railway, and a trolley passenger's nickel fare entitled him to admission to the park. Water from the famous "spring" was said to have healing powers and was eagerly sought by residents suspicious of the city's drinking water. The park was sold in 1921 to G. Russell Dettor who added a large swimming pool there. It later became a private club.

Taylor's Groceries

This small grocery store was established around 1890 to serve the neighborhood of Grady Avenue. It continues to this day as a "convenience store." Mr. Taylor kept the store for many years, helped out by his three children when needed. It was later operated by R. J. Sellers, and in the late 1940s it became Gentry's Market. The store carried everything a woman needed in a hurry. For years, small children would trail in with grocery lists for their mothers. Since there was little in the way of refrigeration at the time, and no supermarkets, families depended on the neighborhood grocery store for most of their "store bought" goods. After WW II, improved refrigeration and transportation encouraged the development of chain stores, and the supermarket pushed many neighborhood markets into oblivion.

Bridge of Scores

In the first years of the 20th century University Avenue was dug out, the banks graded, and this trestle was built over the road. No sooner, it seems, was construction completed, than students began advertising the University's football and baseball achievements on the bridge and its abutments. This 1906 photograph shows that the University athletic teams were very successful against Ivy League teams. Note in the background the old gates of the east entrance to the Grounds, and the high bank along University Avenue. The end of brick-paced Main Street shows the boundary between the city and the county. It was not until after 1916, when Charlottesville annexed this area from Albemarle County, that the rest of the street was improved. The sidewalk along the Corner was built in 1902.

Corner Businessmen

This 1917 photograph shows some of the leading businessmen on the University Corner posed in front of Anderson Bros. Bookstore. At the extreme left is Dr. William Sheppe, who owned the University Drug Store. Next is R. M. Balthis, the manager of Anderson's, and his son, Alphonse. With the glasses is J. H. Irving, who with Harry Robinson (fifth from left) owned the grocery store. The man with the pipe is Capt. Snyder, who sold newspapers on the Corner. In the foreground stands A. T. Jameson, the assistant manager of Anderson's. Jameson later left Anderson's and opened his own bookstore on the Corner in the building where Lloyd's Rexall is today. The men in the white coats are Charlie and William Brown, who operated a barbershop under the poolhall. Between them stands Henry Martin, the bell-ringer for the University.

Anderson Brothers Book Store

Anderson's is the oldest business in the city in the same location where it originally opened. The original 1848 building shown here housed a tailor shop and, later, a bookstore. Richard Dabney Anderson bought the bookstore in 1876 and was joined in business by his brother, John. In 1881 the name was changed to Anderson Brothers. R. D. Anderson helped Dr. William A. Lambeth begin the athletic program at the University, and for his contributions he was later named "Father of Athletics" at the University. His grandson, John W. Williams, operates the business today. In 1888, the bookstore had what is reputed to be the first commercial telephone in Charlottesville. The present building was constructed in 1891 around the original structure and has been renovated several times.

University Billiard Parlor

This elegant billiard parlor was located on the Corner where Victorius Framing Shop is today. The proprietor, John LaRowe, is shown leaning against the chair rail in this 1912 photograph. LaRowe was also an enormously successful boxing instructor at the University for nearly twenty years. LaRowe promoted exhibition matches here, and some of the leading eastern billiard champions met on these tables. Note the brass cuspidors, thoughtfully provided for tobacco-chewing customers. In 1926 LaRowe moved his establishment into new quarters built by the Anderson Bros. company off the alley behind the Corner. At the time it was the largest poolroom in the South. The poolhall continued to be a popular place for students' amusement until the last decade.

Temperance Hall

Funds donated to the Sons of Temperance, an organization at the University dedicated to abstinence, paid for the construction of this building in 1856. The second floor assembly room was the meeting place for the Sons until the temperance movement died out after the Civil War. A 1912 donation of $20,000 by Mrs. Charles Sneff was marked for the improvement of the east entrance to the Grounds. The plans included the razing of Temperance Hall. When the hall was demolished in favor of the Sneff Gates, the bookstore moved into a brick building which was built just to the east of the hall. In 1963 the University Bookstore moved again, into quarters across the street. This 1913 photograph also shows a portion of the original University Hospital (left background) established in 1901.

University Tea Room

Miss Thurmond opened the tea room sometime before WW I in the west wing of the building that now houses the Student Health Clinic. The University Bookstore was located next door. This building was originally located a little further west on University Avenue, but in the early 1920s the building was jacked-up and moved closer to the C. & O. bridge. In the 1920s the Nance sisters took over operation of the tea room. The kitchen served three meals a day, seven days a week. Meals were normally served on a contract basis by the month, although a meal could be had at any time at individual cost. The monthly contract was very popular with students. The food served at the tea room was said to be delicious, and the prices were certainly reasonable by today's standards—a fine meal cost 35 cents.

The first streetcar line in Charlottesville began operation in 1887. The line ran from the Charlottesville & Ohio Depot to the University Post Office. Power was supplied by two horses, or mules, and an extra mule was kept at the foot of Vinegar Hill to help make the steep climb. Once at the top, the unharnessed mule would return to the foot of the hill on his own to await the next car. The four-car line, called the Charlottesville and University Railway, prospered for several years until 1894 when a competing electric-car line was built, paralleling the original animal-powered route. The two lines operated independently for about a year, then they merged and the horse-car line went out of existence. R. P. Valentine, the chief owner of the horse-car line, became one of the directors of the new Charlottesville City and Suburban Railway. The first electric cars were open, and to keep drivers from violating the city speed limit they were equipped with a device which rang a bell when the car exceeded ten miles per hour. The nickel fare was maintained. Just before 1900 the railway began to expand. A line was extended down Jefferson Park Avenue to a loop located at Fry's Springs Park, where there was a hotel, theater, and dance pavilion, all operated by the trolley company. The price of admission was the five cent trolley fare. Company plans to expand the line onto the University Grounds were thwarted by student and faculty protest. In 1900 the railway merged with the local gas and electric utility in an attempt to increase its revenue from sources other than the streetcar line. However, the financial situation did not improve. Rising operating expenses and increased taxes forced the company to be sold at public auction in 1903. The railway was bought by a committee of bondholders, and a new company, the Charlottesville & Albemarle Railway, was chartered. At this time the line had 3.4 miles of track, and operated four closed cars and one open car. In 1912 the line was extended up University Avenue to Madison Hall and four additional cars were put into operation. The new cars were painted orange and blue, the colors of the University. Two years later the line was extended to Rugby Road to the C. & O. overpass where a loop was constructed. This brought the railway to a total of 3.5 miles of track. During the prosperous years of World War I and the 1920s, the company ran profitably, but each year it lost more business to the competing automobiles and motor-buses. The railway declined sharply after 1925, and after 1932 it was operating at a deficit. In 1935 the Virginia Public Service Company, which had bought the trolley line in 1926, abandoned the electric cars and substituted bus service. Most of the conductors became bus drivers for the new line.

Charlottesville and Albemarle Railway

Pageant of Democracy

America was at war on July 4, 1918 when this elaborate pageant was staged at the University. Over 3,000 local citizens crowded onto the Lawn to watch the symbolic defeat of the Forces of Darkness. The blare of trumpets announced the coming processional, and the Albemarle County Rifles, the Boy Scouts, Red Cross workers and school children marched down the Rotunda steps. A second blare of trumpets brought the players into action. Civilization, Autocracy, and dancing girls approached the stage. Civilization was enthroned and "America" was sung. Some 78 actors in all participated under the various guises of Belgium, Joan of Arc, Democracy, Truth, Justice, Liberty, the Allies, and the Oppressed Peoples. The proceeds from the event went to the Red Cross.

Unveiling

On Founder's Day 1915, Karl Bitter's statue of Thomas Jefferson was presented to the University. President Edwin Alderman led a procession of some 800 students and faculty in the ceremonies. The main address was given by Fairfax Harrison, president of the Southern Railway. The statue, a gift of Charles R. Crane, was formally presented by David F. Houston, the Secretary of Agriculture. A direct descendant of Jefferson, "Willie" Randolph, pulled the unveiling cord and placed a wreath of immortelles at the figure's feet. In accepting the statue, President Alderman said, "It will present to the eyes of endless generations of youth the face and form of Thomas Jefferson in his old age... mind and heart on the task of building here an institution fit to train the youth of a democratic society."

STUDENTS, FACULTY AND STAFF of the University of Virginia were called for work and classes by the tolling of "Uncle" Henry's bell for more than half a century. The following conversation with Uncle Henry was printed in the Corks and Curls, *the yearbook of the University of Virginia in 1914, the year in which this picture was taken. In the old days, the bell was located outside, above the South Portico on the Rotunda. Today the time is marked by electronic chimes in the University Chapel.*

I dun know why they named me Henry Martin. Ole Missus git it out'n the book. I was born on fo'th day of July, 1826, the day Mr. Jefferson died. Colonel William Cyarr bought me when Monticello was sold. My mother belonged to Mr. Jefferson. She married his body-servant. Cose I don't remember Mr. Jefferson, but I remember my mother and she was a good woman. I been connected with the University sense I was nineteen years old, but not 'fically connected with it till they made me bell-ringer. Yes, sir, I was bell-ringer at this University for fifty-three years, and I been as true to that bell as to my God. Bell-ringin' don't mount to much now. I sometimes think the University'd go right on if they didn't have no bell. Up to the Surrender I rang it at fo' o'clock every mornin'. After the Surrender I rang it at ha'f pas' fo', then at five. It means somethin' for a man to ring a bell continuous at this University for fifty-three years. Now as I come to think on it, I did miss one mornin'. Right after the Surrender the students climbed up and turned the bell over and poured it full o' water. They didn't mean no disrespec' to the bell but it froze and cracked. They got me a new bell then, but it ain't never sounded to me like the old one. All the folks 'round here listened for my bell and went to work by it. Durin' the war I nursed hundreds of students right there in the Rotunda; and when I go in now, I'm thinkin' on the soldiers that I seen layin' on the floor. It didn't make no difference how much they was sufferin'; they didn't make no noise. No, sir, they lay right still a-lookin' straight up at the ceilin'. This bell they got now, it sound just the same for a funeral as for a game o' football; but when I rang the old bell befo' the Surrender, everybody knew just as soon as they heard it what I was ringin' it for. I heard all the Bible lectures of Dr. McGuffey and Mr. Minor. I learned more from them lectures than a colored man every gets out'n readin' and writin'. I learned that when it eases your mind to do a thing, it's right; and when it don't ease your mind, you better go slow.

Henry Martin

Rotunda with Annex

The Rotunda was designed as the focal point of Thomas Jefferson's "Academical Village." It housed the University's library and served as a lecture hall. In 1851 an annex was added to the Rotunda to alleviate the shortage of classroom space. Inside the Annex was the largest auditorium in Charlottesville. The hall had galleries on three sides which, including the floor space below, provided seating for 1200 spectators. At one end of the hall hung a copy of Raphael's "School of Athens" by Paul Balze. The annex was never included in Jefferson's plans for the Lawn, and when the building was destroyed by fire in 1895 it was never rebuilt. The pond in the foreground provided water and ice for the University, and was located where the University Chapel is today. This photograph was taken before 1889.

The Great Fire

JUST BEFORE 10 O'CLOCK on the morning of October 27, 1895 a student noticed a thin wreath of smoke coming from the northwestern end of the Annex. The startled student ran to inform Henry Martin who jumped to his bell-rope and sounded the alarm. Students and faculty, led by Prof. William H. Echols, rushed to the scene. They broke down the door to the Annex and entered, only to discover the Hall filled with smoke and the great painting, the "School of Athens," in flames. Neither the University nor Charlottesville had enough firefighting equipment, and an attempt to form a bucket brigade was thwarted by the massive cloud of smoke. The Annex was given up for lost, and unless something was done quickly, the Rotunda would be destroyed, also. The flames, fed by a strong southward wind, were already spreading across the connecting bridge from the Annex to the Rotunda. Prof. Echols, armed with one hundred pounds of dynamite, attempted to destroy the connecting bridge. He succeeded in bringing down several pillars, but the bridge held. While additional explosives were being procured, students and townspeople were hurriedly removing books from the library in the Rotunda. Load after load of books was dumped from the windows overlooking the south portico into blankets and sheets held below to catch the volumes. Braving the smoke and flames, Prof. Echols climbed out on the dome and coolly hurled fifty pounds of dynamite on the connecting roof. The resulting explosion was said to be heard fifteen miles away. The Rotunda rocked and every pane of glass was shattered; the crowd of people in the library, convinced the building was about to collapse, rushed for the door. However, the connecting roof remained intact and the flames advanced. Meanwhile, the authorities of the cities of Lynchburg and Richmond dispatched special trains loaded with fire engines and firemen to the scene. Unfortunately they did not arrive in time. It became clear that the Rotunda was lost, and the next matter of concern was saving the rest of the buildings on the Lawn. Undaunted, Prof. Echols dynamited the two wings which joined the Rotunda with the Lawn. However, a sudden shift in the wind from north to south walled back the flames and saved the rest of the Lawn. At one o'clock the dome of the Rotunda collapsed, ending the chance of any further spread of the flames.

The Great Fire

After the Great Fire

Courtesy of the Department of Special Collections, University of Virginia

The Rotunda before the Great Fire, South Portico

The Rotunda as the Library after the Great Fire

"Uncle Peter" was one of several community figures visible around the University at the turn of the century. Occasionally, he gardened and did odd jobs, and other days he haunted the Grounds, where a student described him:

"An ebony skinned darky, grown hoary in years of service, an antique specimen of that almost forgotten type—the antebellum slave. Bent by age, wrinkled by exposure, clad in some professor's cast off coat, always wearing a hat and supported by a gnarled hickory stick, he was as inevitable as the baseball defeats of late. Seated on a coal box in the arcade of the East Range basking himself in the rays of the noontide sun, Uncle Peter becomes in first class trim to narrate stories of those halycon days just 'befo de Wah'. His accomplishments are very few, his favorite occupations seem to be doffing his hat, requesting a dime, or purloining coal. He was a natural actor in his capacity to attract the eye, wearing his rags with style and, when persuaded to 'cut the buzzards wing' (a dance) which he did rarely and never without some money paid in advance, he would go through a maze of intricate steps—no doubt African in origin—waving as to soar with his arms and rags, until the buzzard was soaring down; and then he tilted on one foot and scraping on the ground with the other in almost a circle, the buzzard wing arms swung low, then dropped. It was almost hypnotic and when he had caught his breath, the hat was off, the mouth wide open and another contribution was in order. With all the apparent poverty he owned a house "down in the bottom," with a nice fence and gate, and had a fat disagreeable wife and a lazy daughter. I fear he got slim pickings in that household."

Uncle Peter

Montessori School

In the early part of this century the Montessori method of teaching small children came to this country. Miss McLester learned this new approach in Italy and brought it back to the University of Virginia. A Montessori school applying the new educational techniques was established on the West Range of the University Grounds. This 1912 photograph shows the kindergarten in action; the children are given playthings that encourage logical curiosity—blocks that fit together, puzzles, and larger numbers to place in sequence. While the Montessori approach's emphasis on development of a child's initiative may seem unoriginal today, it was a marked departure from most previous ideas on education. The building in the left background is the old medical building and Anatomical Amphitheater.

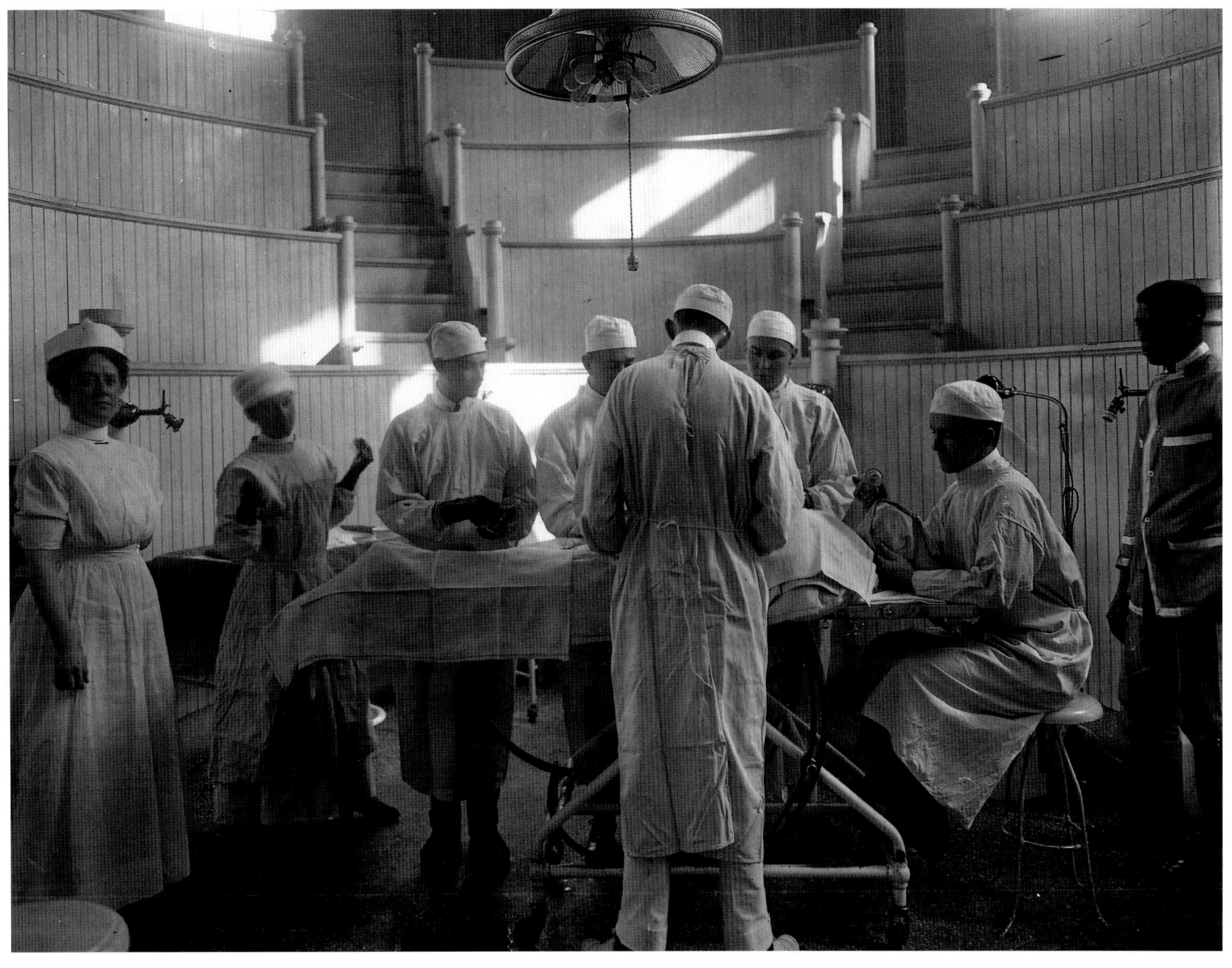

Anatomical Amphitheater

This unusual photograph, *ca.* 1910, shows surgeons at work in the Anatomical Amphitheater. Thomas Jefferson designed the gallery so the interior would be well lighted. The fan-shaped windows were placed well above eye level so the public could not peer in. To allow as much natural illumination as possible, there was also a skylight in the middle of the room. The building burned around 1886, but was restored and continued to be used as the medical school until University Hospital replaced it. It was then used as a classroom and later as the School of Rural Economics. The Amphitheater has the dubious distinction of being the only Jefferson-designed building to be demolished. It was located on McCormick Road, behind West Range and it was torn down in 1938 to make room for Alderman Library.

"Chateau Front and Back"

This cottage was located at the intersection of Ivy and McCormick Roads near the northeast corner of the present Alderman Library. It was built in 1856 by William A. Pratt, the University's superintendent of buildings and grounds. Later, when the University Chapel was built, the cottage was faced with stone and given its gables to match the Gothic Revival design of the Chapel. After Mr. Pratt's tenancy, the lodge became the residence of Henry Martin, the University's bell-ringer. The cottage continued to be occupied, mostly by faculty members until 1937 when it was demolished to make room for the new library. Because of its design and the drawbridge over the surrounding dry moat, the lodge was nicknamed "Chateau Front and Back," derived, perhaps, from the Chateau Frontenac in Quebec.

Student Army Training Corps

In 1918 the new draft law threatened to empty American colleges of their students. This problem was solved by the creation of the S.A.T.C., which resulted in the enlistment of virtually the entire student bodies of most colleges into the Army as a special corps. This scheme allowed students to stay in college while receiving the military instruction as well as remaining liable to service in the regular army. By autumn the corps was organized and military drills had begun. Then fate struck. The influenza epidemic forced the corps to cease operations. By the time the quarantine was lifted, the Armistice was signed. The Corps Commander wrote later that "the good men volunteer, and [that is] why conscription is absolutely necessary to avoid killing them all off." This photograph was taken on Rugby Road.

Lyndhall Apartments

Housing, it seems, has always been in short supply for University students. The Lyndhall Apartments, built in 1914, was one of the first apartment houses to be built in the city. Until then, it was common for families to take students and teachers into their homes as boarders. The Lyndhall, located at 64 University Circle, was built by Mrs. J. H. Lindsey and Mrs. Hallquest. The apartments were built as "non-housekeeping" apartments—that is, they had no kitchens. Instead there was a huge dining room on the first floor which served the tenants as well as students from nearby fraternities. This photograph shows the kitchen, located in the basement, which served some 100 people per meal. The kitchen was furnished with the best equipment of the day. In 1937 kitchens were added to individual apartments.

"The Lodge"

This *ca.* 1917 photograph shows the elegant interior of Charlottesville's first country club. Built in 1916, the house is located at "Trail's End" off Rugby Road, not far from where Cochran Park was. The club had dining facilities, a swimming pool, a large patio, and large, well kept lawns. For a little more than a decade, beginning in the mid-1930s, the house was the private residence of James M. Rothwell, owner of the Rothwell Storage and Ice Co. In 1948 it became the home of the Chi Psi fraternity, one of the nation's oldest fraternities. Chi Psi was originally established at the University in 1860 but became inactive after the Civil War. After several unsuccessful attempts, house was re-established after World War II. Chi Psi had the first House-mother of any University fraternity.

Flying Machine

Less than a decade after the Wright Brothers first success, the citizens of Charlottesville saw the miracle of aviation themselves at a flying exhibition in Lambeth Field on April 6, 1912. Fighting an irregular, twenty mile an hour wind, Beckwith Havens piloted a Curtis Bi-plane to the delight of 5,000 spectators. At 2 o'clock the daring young aviator ascended. He attained a maximum height of about 1800 feet and covered some fifteen or twenty miles. He reached speeds of up to 75 miles an hour during his ten minute flight. After a half hour rest, Havens took off again, barely clearing the tree-tops, *The Daily Progress* reported that "cheer after cheer arose from many parts of the grounds" as the plane sailed over the University. A third scheduled flight was cancelled because of unfavorable weather.

Cochran Park Show Grounds

Cochran Park was located between the north end of Rugby Road, the 250 Bypass, and Route 29 North. This August 2nd–3rd, 1916 horse show attracted the largest opening day crowd in the park's history up to that time. No doubt some of the one thousand spectators were attracted by the racing card on the program. There were nineteen showring events and five races, and horse fanciers and participants came from all over the state for the competition. The races featured Combination, Harness and Saddle Horse, Green Hunters, Ladies' Harness Horses, Heavy and Middle Weight Hunters, Thoroughbred Hunters, Roadsters, the Merchant's Cup, and the Corinthian Class. The first race was a free-for-all, the second was a farmer's race, the third for hacks and hunters, the fourth was a free-for-all, and the fifth was a free-for-all steeplechase.

Memorial Gymnasium

This photograph and the one on the next page are part of the same panoramic view taken from Carr's Hill. The Memorial Gymnasium was built in the early 1920s, and dedicated to the University students and alumni who served in World War I. It replaced Fayerweather Gymnasium as the major University athletic facility, and at the time, it was the third largest gymnasium in the East. Although it has been superceded by University Hall, it still houses intramural sports. The reflecting pool was drained in 1952.

Emmet Street & Ivy Road

As the photograph shows, the country was quite a bit closer to the University than it is now. The tree-lined road to the left is Emmet Street, or Route 29. The tiny lane between the cluster of houses is now Route 29 North. As one can see there was no more than a trail leading over the railroad tracks. The open land in front of the gym is now the site of the Lady Astor tennis courts. Needless to say, this dirt lane is now a major highway.

"The Muleskinners"

The Virginia legislature authorized state convicts as a source of labor for road work in 1906. The first convict camp was established in Goochland County. Camp 15 was established in Albemarle County in 1911 with forty-three inmates (36 blacks, 7 whites). This 1913 photograph shows the camp inmates in front of their quarters. The camp was located on old Ivy Road near Charlottesville. The labor force of this camp was known as "the Muleskinners" because of their pride in working hard. They bragged they were able to cut four miles of trees per day. Particularly notorious prisoners, and those with records of escape attempts were kept in the state prison. Only the trustworthy were allowed in the road camps. The striped uniforms were eliminated in the 1920s, and the chaining of prisoners was abolished in 1953.

Apple Picking

Agriculture was the major industry in Albemarle County when this picture was taken, and the "Albemarle Pippin" was a famous fruit. The Pippin was the product of a graft from a New York tree to the native Albemarle crab apple. In 1838 the American ambassador to the Court of Queen Victoria, Alexander Stevenson of Albemarle County, introduced the Pippin to the Mother Country. His wife reported that "they were eaten and praised by royal lips, and swallowed by many aristocratic throats." The apples "created a great sensation at the palace; that it had been feared they would have been the death of the Premier, Lord Melbourne, who after the Queen retired, had actually eaten two of immense size, and that all who had seen him perpetuate the rash act had considered him a dead man."

Confederate Veterans' Reunion, June 24, 1931, in front of Albemarle County Courthouse

Courtesy of the Department of Special Collections, University of Virginia

RESOURCES

Books

Alexander, James. *Early Charlottesville Recollections 1824–1874.* Charlottesville: Albemarle County Historical Society.

Bruce, Philip A. *History of the University of Virginia 1819–1919.* New York: MacMillan, 1921.

Cahn, William. *Out of the Cracker Barrel.* New York: Simon and Schuster, 1969.

O'Neil, William B. *Pictorial History of the University of Virginia.* Charlottesville: University of Virginia Press, 1968.

Rawlings, Mary. *Ante Bellum Albemarle.* Charlottesville: The Michie Co., 1935.

St. Clair, Emily Entwisle. *Beautiful and Historical Albemarle.* Richmond: Appeals Press, 1932.

Woods, Reverend Edgar. *History of Albemarle County, Virginia.* Bridgewater, Virginia: C. J. Carrier Company, 1901.

Articles

Barringer, Anna. "Pleasant It Is to Remember These Things," *Magazine of Albemarle County History,* Vol. 24, 1965-66.

Barringer, Anna. "Pleasant It Is to Remember These Things," *Magazine of Albemarle County History,* Vol. 27, 1968-69.

Chamberlain, Bernard P. "Farmington: a History," *Magazine of Albemarle County History,* Vol. 29, 1970-71.

Donohue, Edward M. "From Horse Cars to Buses in Charlottesville, 1887-1935," *Magazine of Albemarle County History,* Vol. 12, 1951-52.

Hench, Atcheson L. "Name 'Albemarle Pippin,'" *Magazine of Albemarle County History,* Vol. 14, 1954-55.

Mopsik, Herold A. "A History of Private Secondary Schools in Charlottesville," (Master's Thesis, University of Virginia), 1936.

Nichols, Frederick D. "A Day to Remember," *Magazine of Albemarle County History,* Vol. 27, 1968-69.

Poindexter, Harry E. "Henry Clay Marchant and the Foundations of the Charlottesville Woolen Mills, 1965-1882," *Magazine of Albemarle County History,* Vol. 14, 1954-55.

Reed, Ralph T. "American Express: Its Origins and Growth," *Newcomen Society* (New York), December 19, 1952.

Shultz, William T. "The Humane Movement in the United States 1910-1922," *Studies in History, Economics and Public Law,* Vol. 123, No. 1, 1924.

Virginia Department of Corrections, Annual Report 1911.

"A Story of Roads in Virginia," Virginia Department of High-ways and Transportation, 1974.

Waddell, Richard E. "The Theater Life in Charlottesville, *Magazine of Albemarle County History,* Vol. 31, 1972-73.

Newspapers

The Daily Progress: Jan. 24, 1903; Nov. 30, 1907; April 8, 1912; Dec. 3, 1912; Aug. 6, 1913; Feb. 10, 1916; Oct. 3, 1917; July 5, 1918; Nov. 11, 1918; Jan. 1, 1933; Dec. 9, 1954; Aug. 10, 1957; April 13, 1962; Aug. 9, 1962; Sept. 21, 1964; June 18, 1971; March 24, 1972; June 15, 1975.

College Topics (student newspaper of the University of Virginia): April 4, 1915.

Corks and Curls (yearbook of the University of Virginia): 1906, 1914, 1919.

Interviews

James Burrus, Beverly Clover, Joanne Phillips Clover, John Dodson, Mrs. Frank Elliot, James Gibson, Mrs. Daniel Griffin, Mr. and Mrs. L. F. Hankins, Ethel Holsinger, Ralph Holsinger, Lionel Key, Linda Johnsen, Annie Lipscomb, Howard Newlon, Flora Orser, Jessie Orser, Nathaniel Pawlet, J. R. Ponton, Marvin Spencer, Mr. and Mrs. Lionnie Vest, John W. Williams, Mütter Woodward Hagerman, T. K. Woods, Mac Woodward.